my
make it you.

sew hip

Easy Step-by-Step Instructions | Unmistakably You Projects | Sewing 101 DVD

Shannon Mullen

Make It You!™—Sew Hip

Text © 2006 Husqvarna Viking, Pfaff, and C&T Publishing

Artwork © 2006 C&T Publishing, Inc.

Publisher: Amy Marson

Editorial Director: Gailen Runge

Acquisitions Editor: Jan Grigsby

Editor: Laurie Baker

Technical Editor: Laurie Baker

Proofreader/Copyeditor: Wordfirm

Cover Designer: Kristy K. Zacharias

Design Director/Book Designer: Kristy K. Zacharias

Illustrator: Tim Manibusan

Production Assistant: Kerry Graham

Photography: Luke Mulks and Diane Pedersen unless otherwise noted

Published by C&T Publishing, Inc., P.O. Box 1456, Lafayette, CA 94549

Library of Congress Cataloging-in-Publication Data

Mullen, Shannon Nina,
    Sew hip : sewing 101 DVD - easy step-by-step instructions - unmistakably you projects / Shannon Nina Mullen.
        p. cm.
    ISBN-13: 978-1-57120-372-4 (paper trade)
    ISBN-10: 1-57120-372-9 (paper trade)
    1. Machine sewing. I. Title.

TT713.M845 2006
646.2--dc22

2006004828

Printed in China
10 9 8 7 6 5 4 3

table of contents

hello!

I want to take this chance to personally thank you for picking up this book and to tell you how *Make It You* got its start.

Sewing has been in my family for many years. My great grandmother taught my mother the fine points of garment sewing and my mom in turn taught me the basic techniques and procedures. I have not only developed this knowledge into a hobby but also a career. As an adult, I have grown increasingly grateful to my mom for taking the time to pass down such useful information.

However, sewing didn't come without a certain frustration. There didn't seem to be many patterns with a youthful twist. This is why we created *Make It You*. Our mission is to promote the creativity and individuality that sewing can bring to you; to give you trendy, chic, fashionable project instructions that you can use on the path to creating the perfect project.

Throughout our lives we live with boundaries. There are rules and perimeters to follow while you are doing everyday things such as driving, cooking, or even writing. Sewing is different. There are concepts in sewing, but there really aren't any rules. There are no sewing police to arrest you for doing something wrong. Sewing is about creativity, expression, personality, and individuality. Making a mistake or straying from the instructions is looked at as a creative opportunity.

Our hope is that you will make use of these project instructions and welcome yourself into a world of endless creativity that will enliven your living space and wardrobe in ways you never thought possible. Take the traditional applications of the different techniques shared in these pages and apply them in a way that is uniquely you.

We wish you the best as you experience these projects and hope you are ready for the creativity you are about to unleash!

So, go ahead, make it you!

Sincerely,

Shannon Mullen

And all of us at Husqvarna Viking, Pfaff, RJR Fabrics, C&T Publishing, and Primedia Enthusiast Group

Supplies You'll Need

Like most hobbies, sewing requires some basic supplies and tools to make the experience satisfying. This chapter will address the general supplies and equipment that you'll need to make the projects in this book. Refer to each project for the specific items needed.

fabric 411

DEFINITIONS

* The finished tightly woven ends of the fabric are the *selvages*.

* Because fabric is woven, it has a *grain line*— threads travel parallel to the selvages (*lengthwise grain*) and perpendicular to it (*crosswise grain*).

* *Straight of grain* refers to cutting or sewing fabric along the grainlines.

* "On the *bias*" refers to cutting or sewing fabric diagonally across the grainlines (fabric is stretchy when you work with cuts on the bias).

* Most fabric has a *"right side"* (the side that is printed) and a *"wrong side"* (the side that is not printed).

* Some fabrics, such as Batiks and solids, are, or appear to be the same on both sides. For these fabrics, you don't have to worry about right or wrong sides.

GENERAL ADVICE

* Fabric is sold by the yard, and you can ask that it be cut in ⅛-yard increments.

* Before using fabric, trim off the selvages.

FABRIC The projects in this book were all made from 100% cotton fabrics designed by RJR Fashion Fabrics. You can use whatever type of fabric you are comfortable working with or that provides the look you want. Be aware that different types of fabrics have different characteristics and may not provide the same look as the projects in the photographs. All of the yardages given for the projects are based on fabric that is 42″ to 44″ wide.

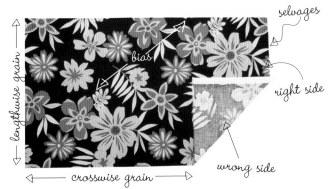

selvages

lengthwise grain

bias

right side

wrong side

crosswise grain

Yardage and Inches

YARDAGE	INCHES	YARDAGE	INCHES
$\frac{1}{8}$ yard	$4\frac{1}{2}''$	$1\frac{1}{8}$ yards	$40\frac{1}{2}''$
$\frac{1}{4}$ yard	$9''$	$1\frac{1}{4}$ yards	$45''$
$\frac{1}{3}$ yard	$12''$	$1\frac{1}{3}$ yards	$48''$
$\frac{3}{8}$ yard	$13\frac{1}{2}''$	$1\frac{3}{8}$ yards	$49\frac{1}{2}''$
$\frac{1}{2}$ yard	$18''$	$1\frac{1}{2}$ yards	$54''$
$\frac{5}{8}$ yard	$22\frac{1}{2}''$	$1\frac{5}{8}$ yards	$58\frac{1}{2}''$
$\frac{2}{3}$ yard	$24''$	$1\frac{2}{3}$ yards	$60''$
$\frac{3}{4}$ yard	$27''$	$1\frac{3}{4}$ yards	$63''$
$\frac{7}{8}$ yard	$31\frac{1}{2}''$	$1\frac{7}{8}$ yards	$67\frac{1}{2}''$
1 yard	$36''$	2 yards	$72''$

SEWING MACHINE A basic sewing machine with a straight stitch and zigzag capabilities is really all that is required. Of course, if you have decorative stitches available on your machine, you can use them to add your own creative touch to the projects.

general instructions DVD!

This book contains complete instructions for all the projects presented. We've also included a DVD with information on all the basic techniques you'll need.

ROTARY CUTTING EQUIPMENT

The rotary cutter has revolutionized the sewing world. It makes cutting pieces easier, faster, and more accurate. The tool looks like a pizza cutter, but the blade is retractable and can cut through many layers of fabric at one time. Rotary cutters come in several sizes. I recommend a rotary cutter with a 45mm or 60mm blade for the projects in this book.

Always rotary cut on a special self-healing mat that is made especially for this task. A rotary cutting mat will protect the cutting surface and the cutter blade. These specialized mats come in a variety of sizes. An 18″ × 24″ mat is a good size to start with. Store your mat flat and away from direct sunlight when you are not using it.

You will also need a rotary cutting ruler to measure the fabric pieces and help you guide the cutter. These rulers are clear and are usually marked in 1/8″ increments. Again, there are many sizes of rulers available. A 6″ × 24″ ruler is a good all-purpose size.

THREAD Good-quality thread is vital to the success of your project. Bargain-bin threads should be avoided. They tend to create a lot of lint, break often, and cause skipped stitches (where the bottom and top threads don't catch each other) and lots of frustration.

Threads come in different weights and fibers. For most of the projects in this book, a 50-weight all-purpose thread made from cotton, polyester, or a cotton-polyester blend should be used for construction. Topstitching thread, which is heavier (thicker), is also used to add a decorative element to several projects in this book. There are many other threads available, such as rayon and metallic, that are wonderful for embellishing.

PINS AND NEEDLES Make sure you have plenty of sharp pins on hand for holding pieces together. Throw away any pins that are bent or can't be easily inserted into the fabric.

The size and type of sewing machine needle you use will depend on your machine, the fabric, and the thread weight. For the cotton fabrics used in this book, the construction is done with an 80/12 sharp or universal needle. Topstitching is done with a topstitching needle, which has a larger eye and thicker shaft to accommodate the thickness of the thread. Use a new sewing machine needle after eight hours of sewing time to prevent skipped stitches or pulling on the fabric yarns.

You will occasionally need a hand sewing needle. Purchase a package of sharps in assorted sizes and you'll be sure to have the one you need to accommodate most woven fabric weights.

IRON AND IRONING SURFACE

Pressing is an important part of sewing. Keep an iron near your sewing area for this task. A portable pressing pad is a good alternative to a full-size ironing board if space is limited. While you may not always use steam, an iron with this feature is recommended.

*pressing 411

DEFINITIONS

* When you *iron*, you move the iron over the fabric in a back-and-forth or sweeping motion.

* When you *press*, you use the iron with an up-and-down motion, holding the iron in place for a short period (3 to 5 seconds).

* When you *press a seam open*, you open the seam up and press the seam allowances to both sides. Often you'll be instructed to press a seam to one side.

GENERAL ADVICE

* You should press, not iron, your seams after sewing.

* If the pressing direction is not indicated in the instructions, press your seams toward the darker fabric so the seam allowance won't show through.

* Pressing a seam to one side creates a stronger seam than pressing the seam open, but pressing it open may reduce bulk and is often used in garment sewing.

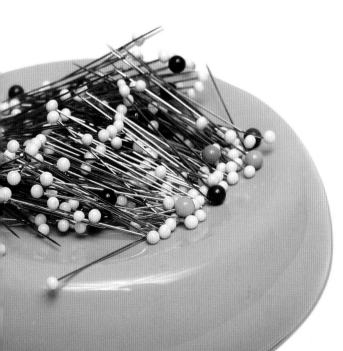

TAPE MEASURE Use a flexible synthetic or fiberglass tape measure for taking accurate body measurements.

SHEARS AND SCISSORS Invest in a good pair of shears for cutting fabric pieces that can't be cut with a rotary cutter. Use these to cut fabric only. A smaller pair of scissors is also handy to have close to your sewing machine for clipping threads.

INTERFACING You can apply interfacing to the wrong side of a fabric to give it support, add shape, reinforce an area, or prevent an area from stretching. It comes in a variety of weights, types, and textures, and can be woven or non-woven, fusible or sew-in.

PATTERN TRACING MATERIAL
Some of the projects require that you trace the patterns from the book so that you can cut the pieces from fabric. While you could trace the patterns onto a piece of paper, pattern tracing material is more stable and can be used many times. You can find it with the interfacings at your local fabric store.

PROJECT GUIDE Watch for these symbols for the degree of difficulty (or ease!) of each project.

MARKING TOOLS There are many devices that can be used to mark fabric. My favorites are a water-soluble marker and a chalk wheel. Always be sure to test the tool on a scrap of the fabric you will be working with to make sure the marks can be seen and then removed.

Mark it up with your favorite marking tool!

EASIEST   **EASY**   **NOT AS EASY**

belts

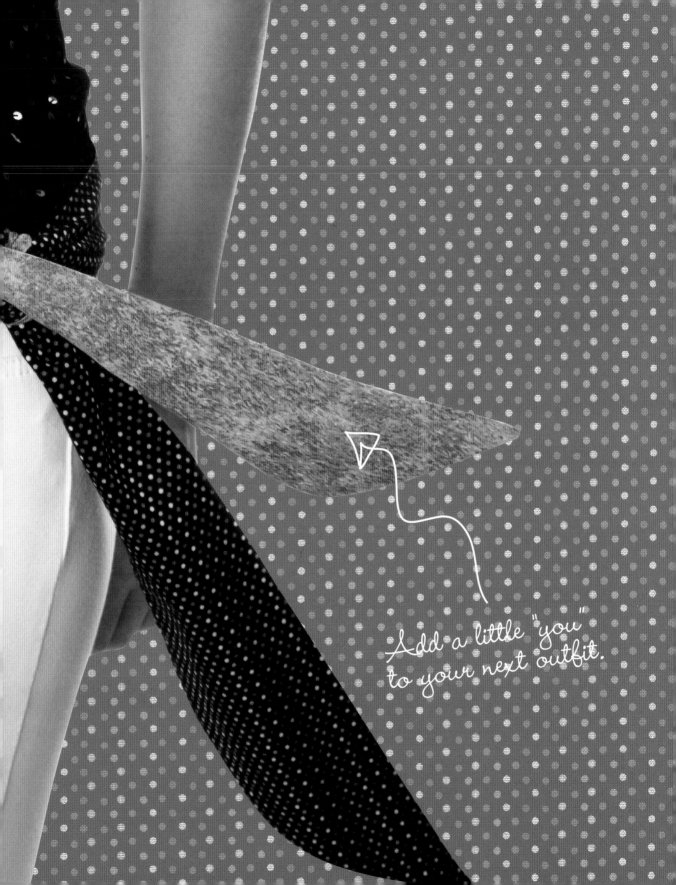

Add a little "you"
to your next outfit.

Raw-Edge Belt

Trendy accessories are the perfect plus to take a plain outfit from boring to flooring. This simple raw edge belt will help you steal the scene with very little effort.

Supplies

FABRIC (see Step 1 to determine the exact yardage)

40-WEIGHT RAYON THREAD in a color that coordinates with the fabric

TAPE MEASURE

ROTARY CUTTER, MAT, AND RULER

SCISSORS

PINS

80/12 UNIVERSAL OR SHARP SEWING MACHINE NEEDLE

IRON

CHENILLE BRUSH (optional)

Instructions

1. Measure around the area where you will be wrapping the belt. Add 9″ to that measurement for the "tails" of your belt. If the total measurement is 40″ or less, purchase ½ yard of fabric. If the total measurement is more than 40″, round up to the nearest ⅛-yard increment and purchase that amount of fabric. For instance, if your waist plus 9″ measurement is 43″, purchase 1¼ yards (45″) of fabric. (See the Yardage and Inches chart on page 9.)

2. Use your rotary cutting equipment to cut 4 belt pieces 3″ wide by the measurement determined in Step 1. For lengths 40″ or less, cut the pieces along the crosswise grain of the fabric (selvage to selvage). Lengths longer than 40″ should be cut along the lengthwise grain (cut edge to cut edge).

*calculating yardage 411

Because fabric is about 40″ wide after you remove the selvages, any measurement up to 40″ can be cut on the crosswise grain. If you need a strip of fabric longer than 40″, you have 2 choices. The easiest option is to cut 1 strip on the lengthwise grain. An alternative is to cut as many strips as you need on the crosswise grain and sew them together end to end with ¼″ seam allowances. The latter option makes sense when the seam won't show and/or when you don't want to purchase the extra fabric.

3. Place 2 belt pieces together, right side to wrong side, aligning the ends and edges. Do the same with the remaining 2 strips. Now, pin the 2 pairs wrong sides together, again aligning the ends and edges.

4. Thread your machine with the rayon thread in the top and bobbin. Select a narrow zigzag or a fun decorative stitch. The stitch should be about ⅛″ wide and complement the fabric without overwhelming it.

5. Sew ⅝″ from the edges around the entire belt. Press the belt.

6. Using scissors, snip the edges every ½″, cutting up to but not through the decorative stitching.

7. Fray the belt edges. To do this, you can either wash the belt or steam the edges with your iron and then rub them with the chenille brush until they are frayed to your liking.

*sewing 411

DEFINITION

The *seam allowance* is the distance from the raw edge of the piece of fabric to the line of stitches. It is often ¼″, ½″, or ⅝″ wide.

So You!

* Make your belt reversible by using 2 coordinating fabrics.

* Use an old broach to pin the ends.

So Fun!

* For a fuller raw edge, use more than 4 layers of fabric.

* Cutting through multiple layers is easier if you use a spring-action scissor designed for rag quilts.

Reversible Belt

You can never have too many belts, but you can conserve space with this simple 2-in-1 version. Just pick 2 great fabrics and you're on your way to one amazing belt.

Supplies

⅜ yard each of
2 COORDINATING FABRICS

½ yard of 22″-WIDE FUSIBLE KNIT INTERFACING

ALL-PURPOSE THREAD in a color that coordinates with the fabrics

TOPSTITCHING THREAD in a color that coordinates with the fabrics

TAPE MEASURE

ROTARY CUTTER, MAT, AND RULER

PINS

SEWING MACHINE NEEDLES: 80/12 universal or sharp; 90/14 topstitching

HAND SEWING NEEDLE

IRON

DECORATIVE BELT BUCKLE

Instructions

1. Measure around the area where you will be wrapping the belt. Determine how long you want the tail of your belt to be and add that to the measurement. Add another 4″ for the buckle overlap.

2. Using your rotary cutting equipment, cut 1 strip 3″ wide by the length of your measurement in step 1 from each of the 2 coordinating fabrics. If the measurement in Step 1 was more than 40″, you will need to cut an additional strip from each fabric; sew 2 matching strips together end to end, using a ¼″ seam allowance right sides together; press the seam open; and then cut each of the pieced strips to the length required.

3. If you want the end of your belt to have a slanted end like the one shown, place the fabric strips right sides together and cut 1 end of the strips diagonally, cutting through both layers at once. Separate the fabric strips.

4. Cut 2½″-wide strips from the interfacing. You will need enough strips to match the length of each of the 2 fabric strips. Follow the manufacturer's instructions to center and fuse the interfacing strips, bumpy side down (the bumps are the glue dots), to the wrong side of each of the fabric strips, leaving the ¼″ seam allowance on each fabric strip exposed, and butting strips together to cover the length.

edges. If desired, sew a second row close to the first row of stitching.

8. Thread the straight end of the belt through the buckle about 4˝. Wrap the end over the buckle center bar. Topstitch the belt end to the belt, using a stretch straight stitch (also known as a triple straight stitch), a reinforced straight stitch, or a zigzag stitch.

5. Pin the strips right sides together. Thread your machine with all-purpose thread in the top and bottom. Insert the 80/12 sewing machine needle. Beginning on 1 long side, sew around the belt pieces, using a ¼˝-wide seam allowance. Leave the buckle end open for turning.

6. Clip the corners and turn the belt right side out. Press the belt.

clipping corners 411

You clip a corner to reduce bulk. To clip a corner, cut off the corner of the sewn angle outside your stitching line, removing extra seam allowance.

7. Thread the machine with topstitching thread in the top and bobbin. Replace the 80/12 needle with the 90/14 topstitching needle. Sew around the belt, ⅛˝ from the

So Fun!

* Use a tube-turning tool (available in many fabric stores) to turn the belt right side out.

* Keep your topstitching straight by using an edge stitching or topstitching presser foot. (Check out your sewing machine's instructions to see if your machine has one.)

So You!

Before you sew the 2 belt pieces together, embellish each strip with decorative threads, ribbons, or stitches for additional interest.

Design-Your-End Belt

Bring out the fashion designer in you by creating the perfect end to your favorite fashion accessory.

Supplies

FABRIC (see Step 3 to determine the exact yardage)

22˝-WIDE FUSIBLE KNIT INTERFACING (see Step 1 to determine the exact yardage)

1 yard of PATTERN TRACING MATERIAL

ALL-PURPOSE SEWING THREAD in a color that coordinates with the fabric

TOPSTITCHING THREAD in a color that coordinates with the fabric

TAPE MEASURE

ROTARY CUTTER, MAT, AND RULER

PINS

SEWING MACHINE NEEDLES: 80/12 universal or sharp; 90/14 topstitching

HAND SEWING NEEDLE

IRON

DECORATIVE BELT BUCKLE

Instructions

1. Measure around the area where you will be wrapping the belt. Determine how long you want the tail of your belt to be and add that to the measurement. Add another 4˝ for the buckle overlap. Round this measurement up to the nearest ⅛ yard to determine the amount of interfacing to purchase. Fabric yardage will be determined after the pattern is drafted. (See Yardage and Inches chart on page 9.)

2. Draw the belt design onto the pattern tracing material. If needed, cut the tracing material in half lengthwise and tape the 2 pieces together to make a piece that is long enough to draw the entire belt. Make sure the buckle end is no wider than the inside of the buckle. The belt shown is 2˝ wide at the buckle end and widens to a 9˝-wide point. You could also shape the end in a point like a sword, round it, or create an inverted point like a fish tail. Do whatever to make it you! Add ¼˝ to the outside edges for seam allowance.

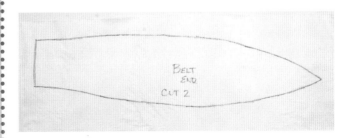

BELT END CUT 2

3. To determine the amount of fabric to purchase, begin with the measurement in Step 1. If it is 40″ or less you can cut out the belt shapes in 1 piece. Measure the widest part of the belt and multiply that measurement by 2. Round up to the nearest ⅛ yard and purchase that amount. For instance, if the length of the belt is 38″ and the widest part is 8″, purchase ½ yard (8″ × 2 = 16″).

If the measurement in Step 1 is larger than 40″, you have 2 options. You can cut the belt shapes in 1 piece or you can sew strips together to achieve the required length. To cut the belt in 1 piece, take the measurement in Step 1, round up to the nearest ⅛ yard, and purchase that amount of fabric. You will have some leftover fabric to use in another project. If you piece the fabric to achieve the length needed, you will need less fabric and have less left over. You will need 2 strips the width of your belt to make each length. To determine the amount needed, measure the pattern at the widest part. Multiply the measurement by 4, round up to the nearest ⅛ yard, and purchase that amount. (See Yardage and Inches chart, page 9.)

4. If you are able to cut the belt shapes in 1 piece, fold the fabric in half, right sides together. If the belt length is 40″ or less, fold the fabric along the crosswise grain (from selvage to selvage). If it is more than 40″ long, fold it along the lengthwise grain (cut edge to cut edge). Pin the pattern to the fabric and cut out the 2 pieces.

If you are piecing (sewing together) the fabric to achieve the required length, cut the fabric into 4 strips slightly wider than the widest part of the belt. Sew 2 strips together end to end using a ¼″ seam allowance. Press the seam open. Repeat with the remaining 2 strips. Lay the pieced strips right sides together, offsetting the position of the seam allowances so they are not on top of each other. This will prevent a bulky spot from being created in your belt. Pin the pattern to the fabric and cut out the 2 pieces.

5. Use the pattern to cut 2 belt shapes from the interfacing, making sure the 2 pieces are mirror images of each other. To do this, cut out 1 piece and then flip the pattern over and cut out the other piece. Trim ¼″ away from the edges of each piece of cut interfacing so there will not be any interfacing in the seam allowance. Follow the manufacturer's instructions to center and fuse the interfacing shapes, bumpy side down (the bumps are the glue dots), to the wrong sides of the fabric pieces.

6. Thread your machine with all-purpose thread in the top and bobbin. Use an 80/12 sewing machine needle. Beginning on 1 long side, sew around the belt pieces, using a ¼″-wide seam allowance. Leave the buckle end open for turning.

7. Clip the corners and turn the belt right side out. (See Clipping Corners 411 on page 22.) Press the belt.

8. Optional: Thread the machine with topstitching thread in the top and bobbin. Replace the 80/12 needle withthe topstitching needle. Sew around the belt, ⅛″–¼″ from the edges.

So Fun!

There's more than one way to make a pattern. If you're feeling really confident about your drafting skills or you have a fairly simple design, use a chalk pencil, chalk marking tool, or water-soluble marker to draw your belt shape directly onto the wrong side of the fabric.

So You!

If you want to add length to your belt without adding fabric, create a tassel effect with ribbons, strips of fabric, or bead fringe.

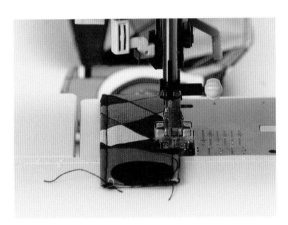

9. Thread the straight end of the belt through the buckle about 4″. Wrap the end over the buckle center bar. Topstitch the belt end to the belt, using a stretch straight stitch (also known as a triple straight stitch), a reinforced straight stitch, or a zigzag stitch.

p

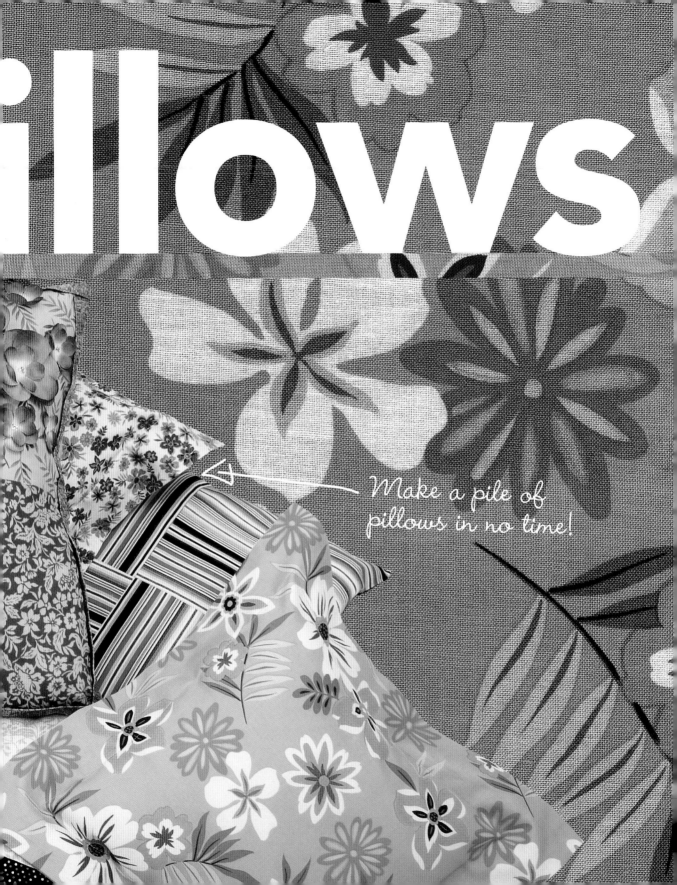

illows

Make a pile of pillows in no time!

Pillow

There has never been a more perfect companion to your style than this flanged pillow. Make several for your bed, for your couch, or to dress up a cozy sitting place.

Supplies

1 YARD OF FABRIC for pillow top and back

ALL-PURPOSE SEWING THREAD in a color that coordinates with the fabric

ROTARY CUTTER, MAT, AND RULER

PINS

CHALK PENCIL or marking tool

IRON

10″ × 10″ SQUARE PILLOW FORM

Cutting

From the fabric, cut 1 square 17″ × 17″ for the pillow front and 2 rectangles 17″ × 12″ for the pillow back.

Instructions

1. To make the back pieces, press under 1 long edge of 1 of the pillow back rectangles ¼″. Press under ¼″ again to enclose the raw edge. Stitch close to the first fold to secure the hem. Repeat with the remaining back piece.

2. Place the pillow front square on a flat surface, right side up. Lay 1 of the back rectangles, wrong side up, on the left-hand side of the pillow front, matching the raw edges. Pin around the outer edges. Place the remaining back rectangle on the right-hand side of the pillow front, matching the raw edges. The hemmed edges will overlap at the center. Pin around the outer edges. Sew around the outside of the layered square, ½″ from the raw edges.

3. Trim the excess fabric away from the corners to reduce bulk. (See Clipping Corners 411 on page 22.) Turn the pillow cover right side out. Press the pillow cover, especially around the edges so they are crisp and flat.

4. Use the chalk pencil or marker and ruler to draw a line 3˝ from each side of the pillow cover to create a square inside the pillow.

5. To create the flange, sew on the marked line, slightly overlapping the stitching at the beginning and end. Pull the threads from the front to the back and knot them. (Gently tug on the back thread until it pulls the front thread through in a small loop. Use a pin or your fingers to catch the loop and gently pull the thread through.) Cut away the excess thread.

6. Place the pillow form inside the pillow cover.

So Fun!

For perfectly pointed corners, when you're stitching the front and backs together take 1 stitch across the point before stitching down the next side. Use a point turner to push out the corners.

So You!

You can decorate the front of the pillow before sewing the front to the back pieces. Any decoration extending to the edge of the pillow will be caught in the seam allowance and secured. For example, weave ribbons across the pillow front. You can also add other embellishments, such as beads or shapes cut out of fabric, by sewing them to the top. Cutting out fabric shapes and using a straight stitch on your sewing machine to secure them to the top (leaving a narrow seam allowance outside the edge of the piece) is called "raw-edge appliqué."

Pieced Pillow Squares

Four compatible fabrics meld into one great project in this easy-to-piece pillow, designed and made by Cate Tallman-Evans. Set on a black background, the squares pop no matter how you arrange them.

Supplies

½ YARD OF MULTICOLOR PSYCHEDELIC PRINT FABRIC for pillow back

¼ YARD OF BLACK PIN DOT FABRIC for pillow top sashing (*strips between the squares*) and border (*strips outside the squares*)

¼ YARD OR 1 SQUARE 7⅜″ × 7⅜″ EACH OF 4 DIFFERENT BRIGHT FABRICS for pillow top

ALL-PURPOSE THREAD to coordinate with fabrics

ROTARY CUTTER, MAT, AND RULER

PINS

IRON

18″ × 18″ SQUARE PILLOW FORM

Cutting

1. From the black pin dot fabric, cut 2 strips 2″ wide across the width of the fabric. Crosscut these strips into 2 strips 2″ × 15½″ and 2 strips 2″ × 18½″ for the border.

Also from the black pin dot fabric, cut 1 strip 1¾″ wide across the width of the fabric. From this strip, cut 1 strip 1¾″ × 15½″ and 2 strips 1¾″ × 7⅜″ for the sashing.

2. For the pillow back, cut 1 strip 12½″ wide across the width of the psychedelic print fabric. From this strip, cut 2 rectangles 12½″ × 18½″.

So You!

Print pictures of your friends onto fabric and substitute the pictures for the bright squares.

Instructions

Sew all pieces right sides together, using a ¼″-wide seam allowance.

1. Sew 1 black pin dot 1¾″ × 7⅜″ rectangle between 2 bright squares 7⅜″ × 7⅜″. Repeat with the remaining 2 squares. Press the seams toward the black pieces.

Sew the black pin dot 1¾″ × 15½″ piece between the 2 units as shown. Press the seams toward the black piece.

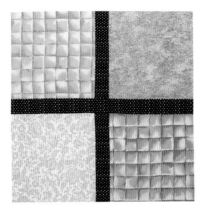

2. Sew the black pin dot 2″ × 15½″ pieces to the sides of the pillow top from Step 1. Press the seams toward the black pieces. Sew the black pin dot 2″ × 18½″ pieces to the top and bottom of the pillow top. Press.

3. To make the back pieces, press under 1 long edge of each of the pillow back rectangles ½″. Press under ½″ again to enclose the

raw edge. Stitch close to the first fold on each rectangle to secure the hem.

4. Place the pillow top on a flat surface, right side up. Lay the 2 hemmed psychedelic print rectangles over the pillow top with the hemmed edges overlapping at the center and the raw edges even. Stitch around the pillow, ¼″ from the edges. Clip the corners and turn the pillow cover to the right side. (See Clipping Corners 411 on page 22.) Press.

5. Place the pillow form inside the pillow cover.

So Fun!

Press the seams toward the darker fabric so the seam allowance doesn't show through the lighter fabrics.

Pillow
Blog Cabin

This pillow is much easier to make than it looks, but you don't need to tell your friends the details. Go ahead and let them believe you're a sewing diva! This pillow was designed and made by Cate Tallman-Evans.

Supplies

1/3 YARD OF BLACK PIN DOT FABRIC for pillow top

1/6 YARD EACH OF BLUE, GREEN, AND DARK PINK PRINT FABRICS for pillow top

1/2 YARD OF MULTICOLOR PSYCHEDELIC PRINT FABRIC for pillow back

BLACK ALL-PURPOSE THREAD

ROTARY CUTTER, MAT, AND RULER

PINS

IRON

18″ × 18″ PILLOW FORM

Cutting

1. Cut 1 strip 3″ wide across the width of the black pin dot fabric. From this strip, cut 1 square 3″ × 3″ for the pillow center. Trim the unused portion of the strip to 2″ wide and cut 2 rectangles 2″ × 15½″.

Cut 1 strip 2″ wide across the width of the black pin dot fabric. From this strip cut 2 rectangles 2″ × 18½″.

Cut 2 strips 1¾″ wide across the width of the black pin dot fabric. From these strips, cut 2 rectangles 1¾″ × 13″, 2 rectangles 1¾″ × 8″, 2 rectangles 1¾″ × 10½″, and 2 rectangles 1¾″ × 5½″.

2. From the blue print fabric, cut 1 strip 1¾″ wide across the width of the fabric. From this strip, cut 2 rectangles 1¾″ × 3″ and 2 rectangles 1¾″ × 5½″.

3. From the green print fabric, cut 1 strip 1¾″ wide across the width of the fabric. From this strip, cut 2 rectangles 1¾″ × 8″ and 2 rectangles 1¾″ × 10½″.

4. From the pink fabric cut 2 strips 1¾″ wide across the width of the pink fabric. From these strips, cut 2 rectangles 1¾″ × 13″ and 2 rectangles 1¾″ × 15½″.

5. For the pillow back, from the psychdelic print fabric, cut 1 strip 12½″ wide across the width of the fabric. From this strip, cut 2 rectangles 12½″ × 18½″.

Instructions

Sew all pieces right sides together, using a ¼"-wide seam allowance.

1. Arrange the black pin dot square and the black pin dot, blue, green, and pink print rectangles as shown below. For each round of strips, the pieces on the sides will be shorter than the pieces on the top and bottom. The strips in each round will be longer than the strips in the previous round.

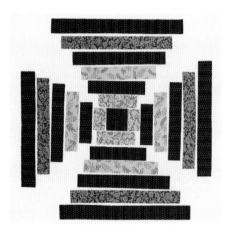

2. Beginning with the first round of blue print pieces, sew the side pieces to the sides of the black pin dot square. Press the seams away from the square. Sew the top and bottom pieces to the top and bottom of the square. Press the seams away from the square.

3. Sew the next round of black pin dot pieces to the blue print pieces in the same manner, adding the side pieces first and then the top and bottom pieces. Press the seams away from the center square. Continue in this manner until all of the 1¾"-wide strips have been attached.

4. Sew the black pin dot 2″ × 15½″ pieces to the sides of the pillow top. Press the seams away from the center square. Add the black pin dot 2″ × 18½″ pieces to the top and bottom of the pillow top.

5. To make the back pieces, press under 1 long edge of 1 of the pillow back rectangles ½″. Press under ½″ again to enclose the raw edge. Stitch close to the first fold to secure the hem.

6. Place the pillow top on a flat surface, right side up. Lay the 2 hemmed psychedelic print rectangles wrong side up over the pillow top with the hemmed edges overlapping at the center and the raw edges even. Stitch around the pillow, ¼″ from the edges. Clip the corners and turn the pillow cover right side out. (See Clipping Corners 411 on page 22.) Press.

7. Place the pillow form inside the pillow cover.

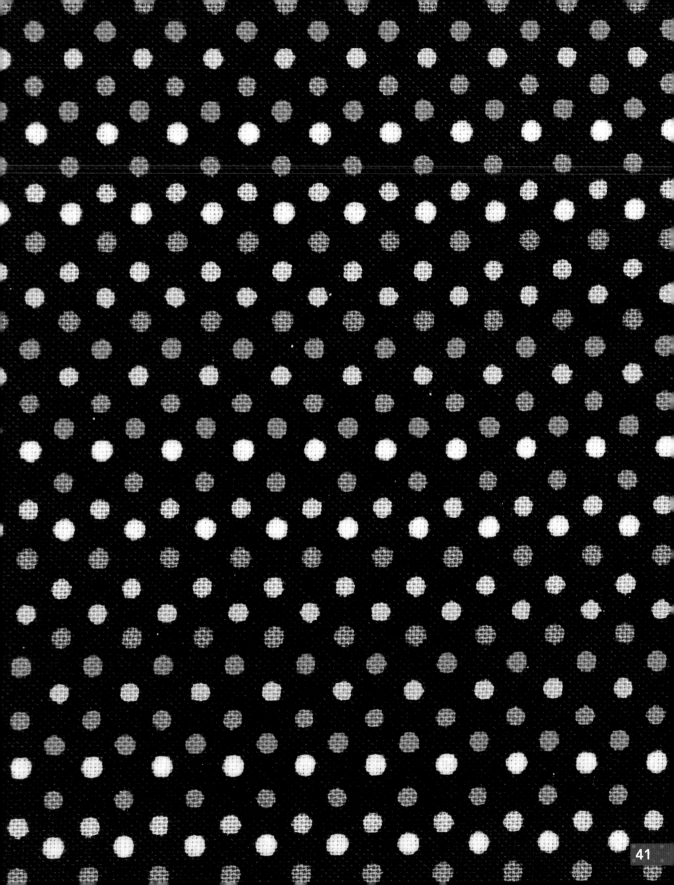

41

Pillow Patchwork

Dress up a simple patchwork pillow with silk flower petals. It's an easy way to add a touch of fun to your décor.

Supplies

⅓ YARD OF GREEN PRINT for pillow front

⅓ YARD OF BLUE PRINT for pillow front

¼ YARD OF PINK FABRIC for flat piping

½ YARD OF COORDINATING FABRIC for pillow back

SCRAPS OF CUT-AWAY STABILIZER or medium-weight nonfusible interfacing

3 BUTTONS, 1¼" diameter

One bunch of SILK FLOWERS that coordinates with the fabrics

ALL-PURPOSE THREAD in a color that coordinates with the fabrics

40-WEIGHT RAYON THREAD in a color that coordinates with the flowers

DOUBLE-STICK PRESSURE-SENSITIVE FUSIBLE WEB (Steam-A-Seam)

WATER-SOLUBLE MARKER

ROTARY CUTTER, MAT, AND RULER

IRON

17" × 17" SQUARE PILLOW FORM

Cutting

1. For the pillow front, cut 1 square 9" × 9" from the green print and 3 squares 9" × 9" from the blue print.

2. Cut 4 strips 2¼" × 18" from the pink fabric.

3. From the pillow back fabric, cut 2 rectangles 12" × 17½".

4. Cut 3 rectangles 2" × 4" from the scraps of stabilizer or interfacing.

Instructions

Sew all pieces right sides together, using a ¼"-wide seam allowance, unless otherwise noted.

1. Remove the flower petals from the rest of the silk flower parts. Separate the individual petal layers.

2. Arrange the petals as desired on the green print

square. Re-layer some of the petals and leave others individual, referring to the photograph if necessary. Be sure to leave enough room around the edges of the square so the petals don't get caught in the seam allowance when the squares are sewn together. When you are pleased with the arrangement, apply a small piece of fusible web to the wrong side of each petal's center. Follow the fusible web instructions to temporarily tack the petals in place on the square.

3. Using a straight stitch and the rayon thread in the needle and bobbin, sew around the center of each individual petal or group of petals, leaving the edges free.

4. Rethread your machine with the all-purpose thread in the needle and bobbin. Sew the flower-embellished square to 1 side of 1 of the blue print squares. Press the seam toward the darker fabric. Sew the 2 remaining blue print squares together in the same manner. Press the seam to one side.

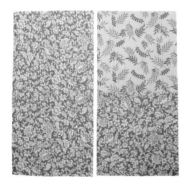

Shown without flower embellishments

5. With the center seams matching, place the pairs of squares right sides together. Sew the pieces together along the long edge. Press the seam to 1 side. This is your pillow front.

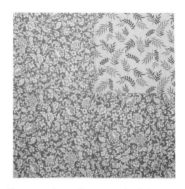

Shown without flower embellishments

6. Press each of the pink $2\frac{1}{4}'' \times 18''$ strips in half lengthwise, wrong sides together.

7. With the raw edges matching, pin a folded strip to the top and bottom of the pillow top. You will have some excess strip extending beyond the ends of the pillow top. Sew along the long, raw edges with a **scant** $\frac{1}{4}''$ seam. Trim the ends even with the sides of the pillow top. Repeat to pin and sew the remaining 2 strips to the sides of the pillow, overlapping the top and bottom strips at the corners. Trim the ends even with the top and bottom of the pillow top.

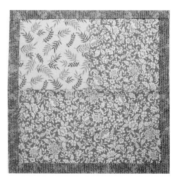

Shown without flower embellishments

8. To make the backing, press under 1 long edge of 1 of the pillow back rectangles $\frac{1}{2}''$. Press under $\frac{1}{2}''$ again to enclose the raw edge. Stitch close to the first fold to secure the hem.

9. Press under 1 long edge of the remaining pillow back rectangle ¼˝. Stitch close to the fold to secure the hem. Press under the folded edge 1½˝. With the water-soluble marker, mark your buttonhole lines 4˝, 8½˝, and 13˝ from 1 short edge. The lines should start ¾˝ from the pressed-under edge and be 1¼˝ long.

2 buttonholes marked

10. Position a rectangle of stabilizer or interfacing inside the fold of the back piece so it is under each buttonhole mark. Stitch the buttonholes and cut them open. (Follow your sewing machine's instructions for stitching buttonholes. If you don't want to sew buttonholes, just eliminate them and the buttons! The 2 back rectangles will overlap.)

11. Place the pillow front square on a flat surface, right side up. Lay the back rectangle with the buttonholes on the left-hand side of the pillow top, right sides together with the raw edges matching. Pin around the outer edges. Place the remaining back rectangle on the right-hand side of the pillow top, right sides together with the raw edges matching. The hemmed edges will overlap at the center. Pin around the outer edges. Sew around the layered square, ¼˝ from the raw edges.

12. Trim the excess fabric away from the corners to reduce bulk. (See Clipping Corners 411 on page 22.) Turn the pillow cover right side out. Press the pillow front, pressing the flat piping out around the edges and leaving it turned inward at the corners. Sew the buttons to the back piece that does not have buttonholes, positioning the buttons so they correspond to the buttonhole locations.

13. Place the pillow form inside the pillow cover and button the cover closed.

So You!

Decorate the centers of your flowers with crystals, buttons, or beads.

So Fun!

Press the seams of the joined squares in opposite directions from each other. The seam allowances will butt up next to each other and your center seam will match perfectly.

bags

Use funky fabrics to make your bag you!

Slouchy Shoulder Bag

Carry your stuff in style! Whether you're going to school or shopping at the mall, this bag will hold it all.

Supplies

¾ YARD OF FABRIC for outer bag and inner pocket

½ YARD OF COORDINATING FABRIC for bag lining

½ YARD OF COORDINATING FABRIC for bag handles

ALL-PURPOSE THREAD in a color that coordinates with the fabrics

6″ LENGTH OF ¼″-WIDE ELASTIC

ROTARY CUTTER, MAT, AND RULER

CHALK MARKER or water-soluble marker

PINS

IRON

SEAM SEALANT

⅛ YARD OF ¼″-WIDE FUSIBLE WEB (Steam-A-Seam)

Cutting

1. From the outer bag fabric, cut 1 rectangle 15″ × 38″ for the bag and 2 rectangles 11″ × 6″ for the pocket.

2. Cut 1 rectangle 15″ × 38″ from the lining fabric.

3. Cut 4 strips 3″ × 38″ from the handle fabric.

Instructions

Sew all pieces right sides together, using a ½″-wide seam allowance.

1. Place the pocket rectangles right sides together. Lay the rectangles on a flat surface with the long edges at the top and bottom. At the bottom of the rectangles, make a mark 1½″ in from each side with a chalk marker or water-soluble marker. Use a large round object, such as a dinner plate, to gently round the sides of the rectangles from the upper corners to the marks. Mark the curve. Cut along the marked lines.

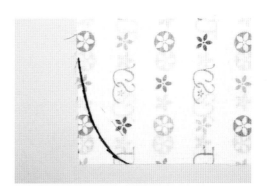

2. With right sides together, sew the pocket pieces together along the sides and bottom edge, leaving the top open. Clip into the seam allowance on the curves, being careful not to cut into the stitching. Turn the pocket right side out. Press. Apply seam sealant to the upper raw edges.

3. Place 1 end of the elastic along the upper edge of the pocket, ½″ from the side and about ⅛″ from the upper edge. Set your machine for a ¼″-wide zigzag stitch. The stitch should just span the width of the elastic. Zig-zag stitch the elastic to the top of the pocket through both layers of fabric, stretching it slightly as you go and ending ½″ from the opposite side.

4. Center the pocket on the right side of the lining rectangle approximately 8″ from the upper edge. Stitch along the sides and bottom edge.

5. Place the outer bag and lining rectangles right sides together. Stitch along both short (15″) edges. Press the seams open.

6. Fold the rectangles in half so the seams are on top of each other. Use a large round object to gently round the corners at the folded edges. Mark the curve with the chalk marker or water-soluble marker. Cut along the marked lines. Stitch along the sides, leaving about a 4″ opening on 1 side. Clip the corners and turn the bag right side out through the opening, stuffing the lining into the outer bag. Press. Use fusible web to close the opening.

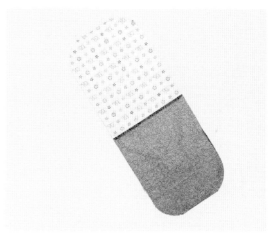

7. Fold down the bag upper edge about 4″ to create a cuff. Press. Using a chalk marker or water-soluble marker, center and mark a 1″ vertical line on the cuff, 3″ from the side seams. Do this on the front and back of the bag. Make buttonholes at each mark, stitching through the bag and cuff. (Follow the instructions for making buttonholes in your sewing machine's manual.)

So You!

Instead of making handles from a coordinating fabric, weave a favorite scarf through all 4 buttonholes, or replace the fabric straps with a pair of ready-made handles.

So Fun!

Skip the hand stitching and use double-stick pressure-sensitive fusible web to close up the openings on the bag and the strap handles.

8. Place 2 handle strips together. Sew completely around the strips, leaving a 4˝ opening on 1 long edge. Clip the corners and turn the strips right side out. (See Clipping Corners 411 on page 22.) Press. Topstitch the opening closed by sewing as close to the edge of the strap as possible along the length of the opening with matching thread. Alternatively, slip stitch it closed by hand. Repeat for the remaining 2 handle strips.

9. Working from the inside of the bag, thread 1 strap through the buttonholes on the front of the bag. Knot the ends on the front. Repeat with the remaining strip on the back of the bag.

Elegant Vintage Handbag

Being practical and fun has never looked so fantastic! This little handbag is perfect for carrying the necessary items, and it doesn't force you to compromise your style.

Supplies

¼ YARD OF FABRIC for outer bag

¼ YARD OF COORDINATING FABRIC for bag lining

¼ YARD OF CUT-AWAY STABILIZER

⅛ YARD OF FAST2FUSE double-sided fusible stiff interfacing

¼ YARD OF DOUBLE-FACED SATIN RIBBON in a color that coordinates with the fabric

ALL-PURPOSE THREAD in a color that coordinates with the fabrics

2 HANDLES OF YOUR CHOICE

PATTERN TRACING MATERIAL

⅛ YARD OF ¼˝-WIDE FUSIBLE WEB

Instructions

Sew all pieces right sides together, using a ¼˝-wide seam allowance.

1. Trace the patterns on pages 54–55 onto pattern tracing material and cut them out.

2. Cut out the bag pieces from the outer bag fabric, lining, stabilizer, and interfacing as indicated on the patterns. Use a water-soluble marker to mark the ribbon placement lines on the right side of 2 of the bag top pieces.

3. Cut the ribbon into 4 equal pieces. Thread each piece through a handle loop and bring the ribbon raw edges together. Pin the ribbon ends to the right side of the marked bag top pieces, aligning the ribbon and bag top raw edges. Baste the ends in place.

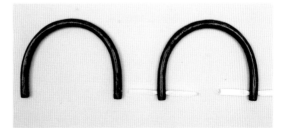

Ribbon through optional wood handles

Basting temporarily holds layers together. You can baste using a long stitch on your sewing machine or by hand sewing, taking big stitches through the layers. The big stitches allow you to easily remove the basting thread. Or take your basting stitches just outside where your seam line will be, so they will be hidden by your final stitching.

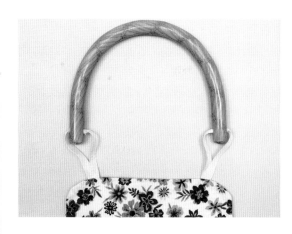

4. With right sides together and the raw edges aligned, place the remaining bag top pieces over the bag top pieces to which the handles have been basted. Stitch ¼˝ from the side and top edges, leaving the long straight edge open. Be careful not to catch the handles in the stitching.

5. Trim the seams to ⅛˝ and turn the pieces right side out. Gently push out the edges with a point turner or a blunt instrument such as a plastic crochet hook. Press. Insert the stiff interfacing piece inside the top pieces. Follow the manufacturer's instructions to fuse the pieces in place.

Connect patterns
on dotted lines

Ribbon
Placement

6. Position the bag body stabilizer pieces on the wrong side of the bag body outer bag fabric pieces. Baste the pieces in place. Place the stabilized pieces right sides together. Sew ¼″ from the side and bottom edges, leaving the top straight edge open. Trim the seam to ⅛″. Turn the outer body piece right side out, gently pushing out the edges with a point turner or blunt instrument. Press.

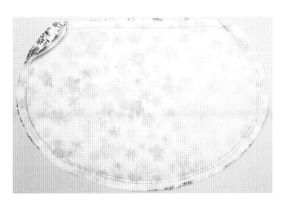

Elegant Vintage Handbag Top Interfacing

Cut 2

Elegant Vintage Handbag Body

Cut:
2 of Cut-Away Stabilizer
2 of Fabric
2 of Lining

Elegant Vintage Handbag Top

Cut 4 of Fabric

Ribbon
Placement

7. Center and pin the bag top pieces along the top edge of bag body, aligning the raw edges. Baste the pieces in place.

8. Place the bag body lining pieces right sides together. Sew ¼″ from the side and bottom edges, leaving the top straight edge open and leaving a 6″ opening on the bottom. Trim the seam to ⅛″. Do not turn this piece right side out. Press.

So Fun!

Cover the stiff fusible interfacing with a non stick pressing sheet when you are applying it to the fabric.

9. Insert the outer bag body into the lining so that the right sides are together. Pin the pieces together along the top edges, sandwiching the top pieces and handles between the body pieces. Stitch along the upper edge. Turn the bag right side out through 6″ opening in lining bottom. Turn under the seam allowance of the opening. Use a piece of fusible web to close the opening, following the manufacturer's instructions. Press the bag.

So You!

Jazz up a great printed fabric with a touch of embroidery. Just use rayon or metallic threads and stitch around the motifs before you apply the interfacing. Or, drop the machine's feed dogs (consult your owner's manual) and "draw" your own designs.

Jazzy Tote

Shop 'til you drop! This roomy tote can accommodate a shopping extravaganza or everything you need for a day at the beach.

Supplies

1½ YARDS OF FAST2FUSE double-sided fusible stiff interfacing

1 YARD OF FABRIC for outer bag and inner pocket

1 YARD OF COORDINATING FABRIC for lining and handles

⅛ YARD OF COORDINATING FABRIC for bag upper edge binding

9″ SPORT OR JEANS ZIPPER

ALL-PURPOSE THREAD in a color that coordinates with the fabrics

¼″-WIDE DOUBLE-STICK PRESSURE-SENSITIVE FUSIBLE WEB (Steam-A-Seam)

WATER-SOLUBLE MARKER

IRON

Cutting

1. From the outer bag fabric and inner pocket fabric, cut 2 rectangles 17″ × 24″ for the outer bag, 1 square 10″ × 10″ for the pocket bottom, and 1 rectangle 2½″ × 10″ for the pocket top.

2. From the lining and strap fabric, cut 2 rectangles 17″ × 24″ for the lining and 2 strips 3″ × 32″ for the straps.

3. From the fast2fuse, cut 2 rectangles 16½″ × 13″ for the bag sides, 2 strips ¾″ × 28″ for the straps, and 1 rectangle 6″ × 17″ for the bag bottom.

4. From the binding fabric, cut 2 strips 2½″ wide across the width of the fabric.

Instructions

Sew all pieces right sides together, using a ½″-wide seam allowance.

1. Attach the zipper foot to your machine. Center 1 side of the 10″ × 10″ pocket bottom square on 1 side of the zipper tape, aligning the edges. You should have ½″ of fabric extending beyond each end of the zipper. Sew the zipper to the square, guiding the zipper foot against the zipper teeth as you stitch. (Refer to the instructions on the zipper packaging or review the instructions on the DVD.)

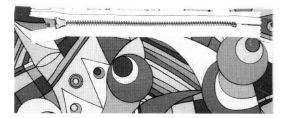

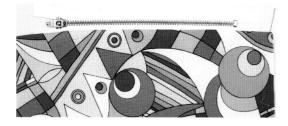

2. Sew the pocket top rectangle to the other side of the zipper tape in the same manner.

3. Press under all the edges of the pocket ½″. Make sure to use a pressing cloth to protect your iron if you are using a zipper with plastic teeth. Apply the double-stick fusible web to the pressed-under edges of the pocket. Center the pocket on the right side of 1 of the lining rectangles. Follow the manufacturer's instructions to fuse the pocket in place. Stitch around the pocket, using a narrow zigzag stitch or the stitch of your choice.

Be careful not to stitch directly over the zipper teeth. Set the piece aside.

4. To make the straps, fold each strap strip in half lengthwise, right sides together. Stitch along the long raw edges. Press the seams open. Turn the straps right side out. Insert a strip of fast2fuse into each strap. Press with a dry iron. Using a zigzag or decorative stitch, stitch down the center of each strip. Set the straps aside.

So You!

Need more pockets? Add different sizes to the lining and or/outer bag pieces before stitching them together.

So Fun!

For best results with the fast2fuse, use a good-quality steam iron and hold the iron in place for a few seconds while steaming.

5. Place the 2 outer bag pieces right sides together. Sew along 1 long and 2 short sides. To square the bottom, open out the bag bottom so the seamline is center and flat, as shown. Draw a line 3″ from the end of the short seamline. Stitch on this line. Clip across the corners, press open the seams, and turn the piece right side out.

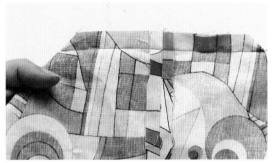

6. Repeat Step 5 with the lining pieces, but do not turn the piece right side out.

7. Position the 6″ × 17″ piece of fast2fuse inside the bag along the bottom. Place the lining piece inside the outer bag piece, matching the seams. Follow the manufacturer's instructions to fuse the fast2fuse in place. Let the fused piece cool before moving it.

8. With the water-soluble marker, draw a line 3″ from each side of the side seams, starting at the top of the bag and ending at the bottom corners. Using a straight stitch and coordinating thread, stitch along the lines through the bag and lining layers.

9. Slide the 16½″ × 13″ pieces of fast2fuse between the bag and lining layers on the front and back of the bag. Follow the manufacturer's instructions to fuse the fast2fuse in place. Trim the top of the bag so that it is ¼″ from the top of the interfacing.

10. Fold the binding strip in half lengthwise, wrong sides together. Press under 1 short end ½″. With the raw edges aligned, position the pressed-under end of the strip at the center back upper edge of the bag. Pin the strip in place around the bag. Trim the end of the strip ½″ beyond the beginning of the strip. Stitch the binding in place. Apply double-stick fusible web to the binding along the folded edge. Turn the binding over the bag upper edge to the inside of the bag. Follow the manufacturer's instructions to fuse the binding in place.

11. Position the strap ends on the front and back of the bag, 4˝ from the sides and 1¼˝ from the bound edge. Zigzag stitch across the raw ends. Stitch using straight stitch just under the bound edge.

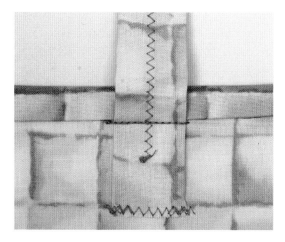

12. Cut several small chunks from the left-over lining and binding fabrics. Randomly place the pieces on the bag front (the side without the pocket) and stitch them in place as desired.

Make a quilt...you!

quilt

Outside the Box Quilt

If you made the Pieced Squares Pillow and Blog Cabin Pillow, you've had a sampling of how the pieces of this quilt will go together. Many of the same elements are incorporated into this 65⅞″ × 82⅛″ quilt that was designed and pieced by Cate Tallman-Evans and machine quilted by Ginger Hayes.

Supplies

3¼ YARDS OF BLACK PIN DOT FABRIC for Log Cabin blocks, sashing, border, and binding

¼ YARD EACH OF LIME GREEN, BLUE, ORANGE, PINK, YELLOW, DARK GREEN, AND MULTICOLOR PRINT FABRICS for squares

1¼ YARDS OF MULTICOLOR PSYCHEDELIC PRINT FABRIC

¼ YARD OF DARK BLUE FABRIC for Log Cabin blocks

⅜ YARD OF MEDIUM GREEN FABRIC for Log Cabin blocks

½ YARD DARK PINK FABRIC for Log Cabin blocks

5⅓ YARDS OF FABRIC for backing

72″ × 88″ PIECE OF BATTING

ROTARY CUTTER, MAT, AND RULER

ALL-PURPOSE THREAD in a color that coordinates with the fabrics

PINS

IRON

Cutting

1. From each of the lime green, blue, orange, pink, yellow, dark green, and multicolor print fabrics, cut 1 strip 7⅜″ wide across the width of the fabric. From each of these strips, cut 3 squares 7⅜″ × 7⅜″. You should have a total of 21 squares.

2. From the psychedelic print fabric, cut 5 strips 7⅜″ wide across the width of the fabric. From these strips cut 1 strip 7⅜″ × 31¾″ and 1 strip 7⅜″ × 24⅞″. Sew the remaining strips together end to end to make 1 long strip. From this long strip, cut 1 strip 7⅜″ × 72⅜″ and 1 strip 7⅜″ × 48″.

So You!

Throw structure out the door and use a different fabric for each strip.

3. From the black pin dot fabric, cut 8 strips 5⅝″-wide across the width of the fabric for the border.

Cut 8 strips 2¼″-wide across the width of the fabric for the binding.

Cut 1 strip 3″ wide across the width of the fabric. From this strip, cut 5 squares 3″ × 3″ for the center of the Log Cabin blocks.

Cut 27 strips 1¾″-wide. From these strips, cut 10 rectangles 1¾″ × 5½″, 10 rectangles 1¾″ × 8″, 10 rectangles 1¾″ × 10½″, and 10 rectangles 1¾″ × 13″ for the Log Cabin blocks. Cut 3 strips 1¾″ × 23⅝″ , 13 rectangles 1¾″ × 15½″, and 13 rectangles 1¾″ × 7⅜″ for the sashing. Sew the remaining strips together end to end to make 1 long strip. From this long strip, cut 1 strip 1¾″ × 49¼″, 1 strip 1¾″ × 24⅞″, 1 strip 1¾″ × 31¾″, and 2 strips 1¾″ × 42⅜″ for the sashing.

4. From the dark blue print fabric, cut 3 strips 1¾″ wide across the width of the fabric. From these strips, cut 10 rectangles 1¾″ × 5½″ and 10 rectangles 1¾″ × 3″ for the Log Cabin blocks.

5. From the medium green print fabric, cut 6 strips 1¾″ wide across the width of the fabric. From these strips, cut 10 rectangles 1¾″ × 8″ and 10 rectangles 1¾″ × 10½″ for the Log Cabin blocks.

6. From the dark pink print fabric, cut 8 strips 1¾″ wide across the width of the fabric. From these strips, cut 10 rectangles 1¾″ × 13″ and 10 rectangles 1¾″ × 15½″.

Instructions

Sew all pieces right sides together, using a ¼″ seam allowance.

1. Refer to Steps 1–3 of Blog Cabin Pillow to make 5 Log Cabin blocks using the black pin dot squares and the dark blue, medium green, and dark pink print 1¾″-wide strips.

2. The quilt top will be assembled in 4 sections. To make section 1, sew a black pin dot 1¾″ × 15½″ rectangle to both sides of a Log Cabin block. Sew a black pin dot 1¾″ × 7⅜″ rectangle to the right-hand side of 3 squares 7⅜″ × 7⅜″. Sew these units together side by side. Sew a black pin dot 1¾″ × 24⅞″ strip to the bottom of the psychedelic print 7⅜″ × 24⅞″ strip. Sew this psychedelic print unit to the top of the squares unit. Add the Log Cabin block unit to the left-hand side of the squares unit. Sew a black pin dot 1¾″ × 42⅜″ strip to the bottom of the section.

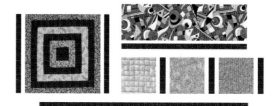

3. To make section 2, sew a black pin dot 1¾″ × 15½″ rectangle to both sides of a Log Cabin block. Sew 2 black pin dot rectangles

$1\frac{3}{4}'' \times 7\frac{3}{8}''$ and 3 squares $7\frac{3}{8}'' \times 7\frac{3}{8}''$ together, alternating the squares and rectangles as shown. Make 2 pieced strips. Sew the 2 pieced strips together, placing a black pin dot $1\frac{3}{4}'' \times 23\frac{5}{8}''$ strip between them. Sew this unit to the left side of the Log Cabin block unit. Add a black pin dot $1\frac{3}{4}'' \times 15\frac{1}{2}''$ rectangle to the left-hand side of this unit. Sew a black pin dot $1\frac{3}{4}'' \times 42\frac{3}{8}''$ strip to the bottom of the section.

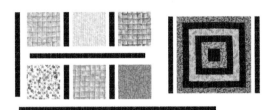

4. To make section 3, sew a black pin dot $1\frac{3}{4}'' \times 15\frac{1}{2}''$ rectangle to both sides of a Log Cabin block. Sew a black pin dot $1\frac{3}{4}'' \times 7\frac{3}{8}''$ rectangle between 2 squares $7\frac{3}{8}'' \times 7\frac{3}{8}''$. Make 3 of these units. Sew 2 of these units together, placing a black pin dot $1\frac{3}{4}'' \times 15\frac{1}{2}''$ rectangle between them. Sew this unit to the right-hand side of the Log Cabin block unit. Sew the remaining unit to the left-hand side of the block. Add a black pin dot $1\frac{3}{4}'' \times 15\frac{1}{2}''$ rectangle to each side of the section.

5. Sew sections 1, 2, and 3 together as shown. Add the psychedelic print $7\frac{3}{8}'' \times 48''$ strip to the left-hand side of the joined sections. Sew a black pin dot $1\frac{3}{4}'' \times 49\frac{1}{4}''$ strip to the bottom of the unit.

So Fun!

If you find that 1 piece is slightly longer than the piece or unit you are sewing it to, sew with the longer piece on the bottom. The feed dogs will ease in the excess fabric.

6. You will make section 4 in 2 parts. To make part A, sew a black pin dot $1\frac{3}{4}'' \times 15\frac{1}{2}''$ rectangle to the right-hand side of a Log Cabin block. Sew a black pin dot $1\frac{3}{4}'' \times 7\frac{3}{8}''$ rectangle between 2 squares $7\frac{3}{8}'' \times 7\frac{3}{8}''$. Make 2 of these units. Sew the 2 units together, placing a black pin dot $1\frac{3}{4}'' \times 15\frac{1}{2}''$ rectangle between them. Sew this unit to the right-hand side of the Log Cabin unit. Add a black pin dot $1\frac{3}{4}'' \times 31\frac{3}{4}''$ strip and then the

psychedelic print 7⅜″ × 31¾″ strip to the bottom of this unit. Sew the black pin dot 1¾″ × 25⅝″ strip to the right-hand side of this part.

To make part B, sew a black pin dot 1¾″ × 15½″ rectangle to the top of a Log Cabin block. Sew a black pin dot 1¾″ × 7⅜″ rectangle between the remaining 2 squares 7⅜″ × 7⅜″. Sew this unit to the top of the Log Cabin unit. Add the black pin dot 1¾″ × 25⅝″ strip to the right-hand side of this part. Sew part B to the right-hand side of part A.

7. Sew section 4 to the bottom of the previously joined sections.

8. Sew the 7⅜″ × 72⅜″ psychedelic print strip to the right-hand side of the joined sections.

9. Measure the length of the quilt to determine the length of the side borders (It will be close 72⅜″). Join the 8 black pin dot 5⅝″-wide strips together end to end to make 1 long strip. From this strip, cut 2 strips for the side borders the length of the quilt.

10. Sew the side borders to the sides of the quilt top. Press the seams toward the borders. Measure the width of the quilt (with side borders) to determine the length of the top and bottom border. Cut 2 strips for the top and bottom borders (it will be close to 66⅜″). Sew the top and bottom borders to the top and bottom edges of the quilt top. Press the seams toward the borders.

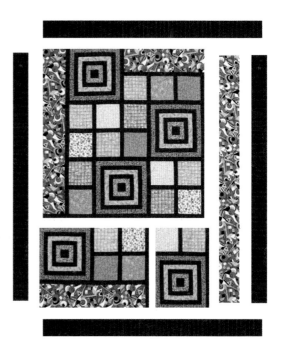

Finishing the Quilt

These finishing instructions are simplified and assume that you have some knowledge of quiltmaking. If you are a beginner, consult one of the many wonderful books on quiltmaking that deal with this subject in depth.

1. Cut and piece the backing fabric so that it is about 6″ longer and 6″ wider than the quilt top. Press the seam open.

2. Place the quilt backing wrong side up on a large, flat surface. Smooth out any wrinkles. Secure the fabric to the surface with masking tape, pulling the fabric taut without stretching it.

3. Center the batting on top of the backing and smooth it out.

4. Press the quilt top. Center it over the batting, right side up, and smooth out any wrinkles.

5. Baste the layers together with safety pins if you are machine quilting and with thread if you are hand quilting.

6. Quilt as desired. (Refer to the DVD for some ideas.)

7. Trim the backing and batting even with the quilt top. Bind the edges with the 2¼″-wide black pin dot strips.

Sources

Check out these places to find what you need to get started!

Cactus Punch
embroidery designs
www.cactuspunch.com
1-800-487-6972

C&T Publishing
fast2fuse®
www.ctpub.com
1-800-234-1114

Coats & Clark
zippers
www.coatsandclark.com
1-800-648-1479

Fasturn
Fasturn Tube Set
www.fasturnjunction.com
1-800-729-0280

Heritage Scissors
scissors
www.heritagecutlery.com
1-800-252-8452

Husqvarna Viking
sewing machines, accessory feet, notions, and stabilizers
www.husqvarnaviking.com
1-800-358-0001

Pfaff
sewing machines, accessory feet, notions, and stabilizers
www.pfaffusa.com
1-800-99PFAFF

Prym Consumer USA
purse handles & belt buckles
www.dritz.com
1-800-255-7796

RJR
fabrics
www.rjrfabrics.com
1-800-422-5426

Warm Co.
batting
www.warmcompany.com
1-800-234-9276

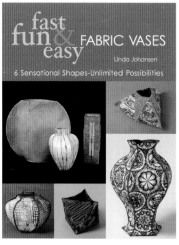